The Hospital Poems

by
Jim Ferris

Winner of the 2004 Main Street Rag Poetry Book Award

MAIN STREET RAG PUBLISHING COMPANY
CHARLOTTE, NC

Cover art by David Chorlton, design by M. Scott Douglass

ACKNOWLEDGEMENTS

The author offers his thanks to Lynn Emanuel, CX Dillhunt, and Stephen Kuusisto for their signal contributions to this book. Thanks also to the many poets, readers, friends who have helped make these better poems and me a better poet. Gratitude as well to the Wisconsin Arts Board, the Mary Anderson Center, and these publications:

Ragged Edge: "Watching Mars," "New Cast,"
    "From the Surgeons"
Comstock Review: "What We Watch"
Paterson Literary Review: "Exercise of Power"

Library of Congress Control Number: 2004114084

ISBN 1-930907-52-4

Main Street Rag
4416 Shea Lane
Charlotte, NC 28227
www.MainStreetRag.com

for Judith
for my family
for all my crip brothers and sisters

and for Laura

I hope these poems

are of use to you.

In solidarity,

Joe

Charlotte
March 2006

CONTENTS

III. The Treatment

Foreword

Disability, most of us may think, is an object of diagnosis rather than an occasion for poetry. Jim Ferris may cause us to think differently. If poetry distills human experience, his precise word pictures render his own early life in ways that will resonate with many readers. In one interview, he called this collection "a memoir in verse," for taken together these poems are, in effect, chapters in a story, his story. They recollect the times he spent as a boy in a rehabilitation hospital undergoing repeated surgeries intended to fix him, to make him more like a "normal" kid. This course of corrective treatments utterly failed to achieve its medical goals, let alone its social ones. It did not make him over physically, it could not make him over socially.

Jim Ferris's boyhood experiences will match the memories of many people with many kinds of disabilities. His poetic memoir will recall to them, not just the physical ordeal of a protracted surgical campaign, but the psychic anguish, the personal costliness, of a program that aimed to refashion a boy into something he never was and never would become, that instructed him he would never be a whole and real person without radical intervention to alter him. Such readers will remember how the most well-intentioned of medical treatments pathologized their very being.

But you don't have to have experienced disability or hospitalization to find yourself in these poems, for the core of the emotional moments they capture are common. The child's sense of being at the mercy of all-powerful adults who impose their will for the child's own good, and are often wrong. The camaraderie of children against adult power. The feeling that one is an orphan abandoned by one's own family. Adult obtuseness in assuming that children have no true sense of dignity and can feel no real sense of humiliation. The realization that one must submit to being made over in order to be regarded as acceptable, which is to say, human and loved. The resistance to all of this, the struggle to define oneself, to develop a sense of pride. The hopefulness and romanticism of youth. Jim Ferris writes, not just from the inside of the experience of childhood disability and hospitalization, but from the inside of all human experience.

If, in one way, these poems express the humanity common to people with and without disabilities, they also implicitly assert that the disability experience, in and of itself, is distinct, significant, and humanly valid. Jim Ferris represents that experience directly, knowingly. This is important because people with disabilities often find themselves talked about and defined by people without disabilities, mostly by people with credentialed expertise. Disabled people are commonly defined by negation, described in terms of what they are not, delimited by assertions of what they cannot be. Ferris shifts the point of view from the outside to the inside. More than that, as he proclaims in the opening poem, he "sing[s] for cripples."

Jim Ferris is not the only "poet of cripples" these days. Rather, he is a leading voice among a generation of poets and playwrights, memoirists and novelists and short story writers, who, like him, are presenting the disability experience from the inside. Many of them are activists as well as artists. In both guises, they are agents in one of the most remarkable transformations in social consciousness in human history: the disability rights revolution. Whenever people band together to redefine their place in the world, creative artists arise among them to express the experiences and perspectives of that group, to render artistically, not just their political agendas, but, underlying those objectives, their personal and collective yearnings and visions. The emergence of a disability arts and culture movement is one such creative upwelling. Though these poems are not overtly political, their unstated assertion of the importance and validity of the disability experience as human experience has vast implications for the political, social, and cultural transformation of which those poems are one expression. For the disability rights revolution is about much more than access ramps and civil rights statutes. It is spurred by, just as it provokes, the most profound questions: What is justice? What is equality? What makes a person human? What is the nature of community? And, of course, what is disability? These are not only questions of politics and public policy. They are at the same time moral and even aesthetic questions. Jim Ferris's poetry does not directly address those questions, but what he has to say is deeply relevant to how we all answer them.

Paul K. Longmore

Poet of Cripples

Let me be a poet of cripples,
of hollow men and boys groping
to be whole, of girls limping toward
womanhood and women reaching back,
all slipping and falling toward the cavern
we carry within, our hidden void,
a place for each to become full, whole,
room of our own, space to grow in ways
unimaginable to the straight
and the narrow, the small and similar,
the poor, normal ones who do not know
their poverty. Look with care, look deep.
Know that you are a cripple too.
I sing for cripples; I sing for you.

I. Child of No One

Watching Mars

At night
you could see Mars
across the railroad tracks—
aliens in white coats doing
God knows

what in
blue-green light. I
guessed they doctored candy
bars on second shift—sometimes Mars
bars would

appear
for us—still, those
days, I never could see
past the white coats enough to tell
for sure.

Normal

Across Oak Park Avenue
is a city park, lush
and busy, where men play softball all

evening, too far away
to watch, their dim voices
drifting across the green. Their cars line

the streets as far
as I can see. Sammy and I,
Robert and I, Hoffmann and I call out

the makes and models
as the cars pass. *Dodge Dart.*
Chevy Nova. We are seldom wrong—*Corvair,*

Pontiac GTO—we who drive
wheelchairs and banana carts—
Mustang, VW, Rambler American—who have not yet

rounded second—
'57 Chevy! My dad had one of those—
who watch out windows a world so soft—*T-bird*—

so fair—*Corvette*—
so normal—*Ford Fairlane*—
a world going on, going by, going home.

Meat

Between four and five they bring down the meat
from recovery—those poor dopes have been simmering
up there for hours, bubbling up to the surface,
blinking, then sinking back into the soup. They're not
like people, exactly, not like the kids we knew
this morning, they've been someplace you can only go
alone, and they come back cooked a little more—
even if the cuts are on old scars, even if
the procedure could be reversed, they are never quite
the same after. If it's your friend you go by his bed
to check on him—if it's not your friend you take a look
anyway—are they back in this world, have they come all
the way back, can you recognize them? Or have they escaped,
have the surgeons cut those tendons and ligaments
that nail us to our spotty selves? When we pass by,
even if we hated the guy, we take care not
to bump the bed. Theirs is a language we all speak.

Patience

The hospital is on a promontory jutting
far out into the ocean. We're on a cliff, about
to topple into the waves which smash against the rocks.
We can't even see across the street—there is no street,
no one can reach us, the thin tongue of land behind us
has crumbled into the sea. Hail drums windows,
thunder rattles the glass until it must break, the lights
go out. The doctors have lit out for shore—we can see
their boat, their white coats in the far distance. The nurses
pound the waves in an open boat behind the doctors,
their white caps serene, protecting them from the weather.
Our island washes away beneath us, wave by wave
it gives us away until we slide down what is left
of the cliff into the alien sea and bob there,
rudderless, our casts and the ether our only friends,
and wait to see what happens next.

The Doctor

English is not his native language.
He says he is a doctor, and they let him practice
on us. He is not like the others with his starched
white coat buttoned all the way up, his trimmed mustache,
his dainty feet. He is gentle in his foreign way.
He speaks softly, and I give him my leg to break.
It hurts, of course, but it's for my own good—
in Europe they do this all the time. When he cuts
a cast off he runs the saw up and down his arm first—
See? It vibrates; it will not hurt you. He breaks
my other leg. It hurts, of course, but you should see
him with a mask on and a scalpel in one hand—
quel magnifique. Bones are, after all, only bones.
I balk at the second arm, but he is the doctor,
and of course he knows best. I am encased in plaster
by the time they take him away. I'm glad
he was so gracious.

Child of No One

Orphaned for the first time
at five—no one died—
Mom just took me to the hospital.
And left. At once I am waif
and ward of the Shrine—damp and trembling
clay to be molded under the sign
of the fez and scimitar.
They issue underpants,
undershirt (sleeveless), white nylon socks,
blue jeans, sport shirt an old man might wear
if he was small and unlucky. All
orphans are equal—all need fixing.

I am allowed to keep my shoes,
one sole thick with cork to make up
for my lack. *Say goodbye, kid. You're*
with us now—inside. And our lives are theirs.
Nurses rule, white-cap commandants
who yield quickly to lab-coat gods
with stethoscopes, scalpels, saws. Chief
divinity is a bald, distracted gnome
with half-glasses tipped on his nose.
Weekly worship, Monday rounds. Parents
unseen, unheard, afternoon visitors,
distant kin who evoke indistinct
images of life outside the orphanage.

But until we make our sacrifice,
until our bodies are corrected,
until the gods deign to let us go,
we are children of no one,
wards of the Shrine, patronized
by jolly mystics in fezzes, orphaned
by our flaws, our families, our fate.

For His Own Good

That first hip spica
must have been tiny,
almost a toy.
Bet I could hold
the whole cast
in one hand—bet
I could hold him
along one arm,
elbow to hand.
I see a kid
that little now
and I wonder
what it must have
been like to
give your baby
to the doctors.
What do you
tell yourself?
What do you
tell the brave
little soldier?

The Question

Like a school of goldfish looking for a handout,
like communicants at the altar rail,
we convene at the front of the ward, open our mouths,
take thermometers under our tongues. I become
FDR with his cigarette holder, but I grant
Miss Barb's demand and slide the thing back under my tongue.
Eventually she comes to me, pinches my wrist—hold still—
pulls the glass from my mouth, reads the mercury, makes
a note on her clipboard, and asks the question. None
of your damned—your *god-damned* business. But I know better
than to say it out loud. I gave the wrong answer once—
under her watchful eye had to swallow a long, tarry glass
of prune juice for my mistake. I choked it down
and learned my lesson: yes, yes, yes. Miss Barb makes a note.

Keeping the Faith

The priest comes early Tuesday mornings;
the night nurse rouses the Catholics,
and we sacrifice our sleep for the joy
of carrying this special cross.
Our fathers are not fond of Freemasons,
of Shriners, our benefactors; maybe that's
why this nondescript priest rises before
the sun: to feed us the faith, to remind
this accidental congregation
in casts and intentional scars
that God still watches, that Jesus
suffered and died for our sins.

Learning the Ropes

Evenings when the Boy Scouts come we tie knots.
Bowline. Half hitch. Two half hitches. Clove hitch.
Running knot, rolling hitch, overhand, square.
Slip knot, sheepshank, sheet bend. The granny knot
is a screwed-up square knot. The scoutmasters
all look alike in their bile-green shirts
as they minister to our need for knots.
We are their good deed for the day. I am
back in Shriners so many times I earn
three Tenderfoot pins but quickly I
forget most of the knots. When I look up
knot in the dictionary I find
a surgeon's knot. We never learned that.
Mostly I remember the square knot,
the slip knot—holding back, and slipping free.

II. Sweet Soul Music

Robert Walton

Robert Walton is from Milwaukee.
He's in a body cast—spinal fusion,
probably. He's the first Negro I've seen
on the ward. He has the loudest voice
of any of us. When he gets angry
he calls you a hoar. I have the best
vocabulary in my fifth grade class,
but I have no idea what this word
might mean so I look it up, puzzle
out the spelling, still can't understand why
he would call me a kind of frost.
When Bobby calls him a nigger he shouts
I ain't a nigger, I'm a nigger-o.

Mercy

A Get Well Soon card as big as a door.
I want to run, but I can't even walk.
And they see me—I am naked and strange,
pinned to my banana cart. Stuck. Dumbstruck.
How did these aliens get in? How can they breathe
in here? This world is not open to you—
leave now, trespassers, you who seek to gaze
on my humiliation. Reid Rooney
and Bob Rosemeyer, stars of the eighth grade,
come from the shelter of suburban elms
to comfort the sick. Blessed are the merciful,
for they shall obtain mercy. But not from me.

Hospital rules—no visitors under sixteen.
They could get in trouble—*I* could get in trouble.
How did you get in here? They show me their passes—
the front desk did me a favor and let in
the enemy. Look away—forget me.
The one you thought you knew is not here—
he doesn't exist. Never did. So be gone,
children. Flee. But they cannot hear the little
I manage to say. They show me the giant card—
who could miss it—and give me the dozens
of little cards from my classmates. I pretend—
thank you—and now they want to play.

We are so strange—I see it all: clothes, casts,
chairs, carts. I pop a wheelie to entertain them.
They are full of questions, and oh God,
take them away, hurt them before I do,
break them and empty their chipper eyes. Forgive
us our trespasses as we forgive those
who trespass against us. Once they leave
I retreat to the still of the linen room
and look out the window until full dark.

The Worst

Traction—never go anywhere,
impossible to hide, can't even close
the door on a stall—piss can and bed pan,
practically out in public. The worst.

Spinal fusion—traction, body cast hip
to skull, the spine stretcher. For thirteen
months. Doesn't get any worse than that.

Spina bifida—on your stomach all
the time, strange thing coming out your back,
tent over your ass, always smell like piss.

How about the kid with the screws going into
his head?

                        How about the one with those little
stick arms he couldn't bend? He couldn't even
speak English. Or the kid who had to stay
in isolation because—well, just because.

I knew a kid in here who had no arms—
couldn't even jerk off.
                                    You jerk off?

No—fuck you.

                        That's what I mean—no loss.
I knew a kid who had no pecker.
Dickless wonder.

                        I had a teacher like that.

You've got no dick and no brains—doesn't seem to hurt you.

Seriously—no dick?

                                        None. That's the worst.

I don't believe it. How does he piss? How does he . . . ?

I'm telling you, that's the worst.

Outpatient

The clinic hives and throbs on the days I come from home
for a checkup. Any day away from school
is welcome, even if it means striding
right up to the edge of the vortex, dangling
one leg in that other world, putting
myself squarely in God's line of sight.
I am not fearless—I am in the building but
still an outpatient. My mother will not leave
without me today. For lunch she takes me
to a restaurant, where I order a BLT.
This is really living—a milkshake too.
When the sandwich comes it is sliced in half, pinned
together with toothpicks. I have never seen this before.

Back in the waiting room we read magazines:
Highlights for Children, Ladies Home Journal.
We read everything in them—Goofus and Gallant,
special advertising sections. As I start
to read *Charlotte's Web* for the eighth time, we are led
to a small room with a padded table and two chairs.
I lie on the table, I read, I scuff my feet.
It is dark outside when the doctor slides back the screen
on this confessional, dark outside when I take off my pants,
dark outside when he diagnoses my transgressions.
I don't measure up, though I try, I try.
A few words with my mother, then he is gone.
I dress, and we trudge home. Penance will come later.

Master Jimmy Ferris
^c/_o Shriners Hospital for Crippled Children
2211 North Oak Park Avenue
Chicago 11, Illinois

I can tell cards from Grandpa Holland just
from the envelope—always "Master
Jimmy Ferris," always the sign for *in care of.*
His handwriting is fountain-pen beautiful,
strong bones, smooth blue muscles—I could never match it—
always urging me to Get Well Soon.
I don't know how to do this. Sometimes
he'll pinch your bare arm and just dare you to get free.
When Momma was little he'd send her out back
to the weeping willow to cut a switch
he'd use on her bare legs. Sometimes his cards
include notes about little things: the weather,
going to the store. Church. Family. Taking a walk.
Always the reminder that I can't quite hear,
that I do not, not really, belong here.

Exercise of Power

The orphanage retained an unhappy dentist who
picked at our fillings and called out to an assistant
where they were. I did not know the code then: a number,
occlusal, mesial, buccal. Amalgam. Each tooth
was mapped by a malcontent cartographer who wore
a pale yellow nylon shirt, buttons off to the side.
Sickly disinfectant was his signature:
mouthwash, deodorant, and cologne. Seldom did he
bother to address us. To get to his yellow room
at the end of the hall we had to pass the nurses'
lounge, the cast room, the recovery room on the right,
and on the left those double metal doors with high windows,
the large green room where no orphan was conscious for long.

Everything seemed so ordinary those quiet days.
But the green sanctum with tile walls was never open—
I could never see much through the glass, never enough
to shake the fear or let me know what really happened
in that room where everyone wore a mask. We were not
to loiter on our rare trips up to the second floor,
but I was drawn to that room, I would have explored it,
I would have hidden away to watch the exercise
of power, the defiance of what God hath wrought,
affirming then fixing divine errors, claiming
a brighter tomorrow for orphans, for cripples, for
those who must suffer for God's mistakes, who must be wheeled
into the large green room to fix what is wrong with us.

Miss Karen

If I dream at all, I dream of Miss Karen.
I am just a teen. I don't remember my dreams.
This leaves me free to construct them throughout the day.
Blonde, tall, especially when I sit in my banana cart.
She is more beauty than I deserve. At night I think of her,
in a stall in the bathroom I think of her. She is my release.

She doesn't wear the usual starched cap; hers is smaller,
a round hat like Jackie Kennedy would wear.
Her white uniform stops just below her knee;
in the center is a dart that points all the way
to a heaven I can barely imagine.

She is married to a carpenter; I hate him. My parents
are nurse and carpenter. I reject my place in this scheme.
Miss Karen cares for me when I return from recovery room.
A few days later my mother asks if she is the one
I think is so pretty. Anesthetic is no excuse—
I have been babbling TO MY MOTHER about Miss Karen.
Mortified, I almost die. Miss Karen saves me.

The Hospital's Milk

I am fat. When I am young, I want to be a doctor.
I want to help people as I have been helped—
I actually say this. Already I am too smart
for the saints. I never want to be a fireman or policeman.
Later I will want to be pope, then president. For now,
I know power when I feel its probing fingers—
this may pinch a bit—and I know what I want.

At twelve I am put on a thousand-calorie-a-day diet. Skim
milk at meals; few sweets. Already I loathe my body;
the hospital supports this conclusion. I eat the food,
but I will not drink this pale proxy for milk. Every day
a full glass of this half milk returns on my barren tray.
Nurses cajole, coax, wheedle, insist, bully; I am
impenetrable. One day after lunch Miss Nancy
calls me into the break room, closes both doors, and hands me
a glass of whole milk. I drink it down. Victory, at last, is mine.

What We Watch

It looks painful—I know it hurts when the doctor
bends my legs like that. And these men show pain—
they grimace, they groan, they pound the floor and moan,
then suddenly they turn the tables, pop the other guy one
or catch him napping and reverse the hold, and the beefy man
who looked like he should have been taken to the hospital
is now the one inflicting the torture. Turnabout
inside the turnbuckles, and T-Bone is my guide.
He's a year older than me, from Michigan, in for some arm thing.
He shows me the ropes, tells me about these marvelous slabs
of marbled meat in tights. There's a war in Vietnam, but we don't watch
the news—we watch Dr. X and Black Jack Lanza,
Larry the Ax and Verne Gagne's sleeper hold
put them out cold, Mad Dog, the Butcher, Moose Cholak,
Baron Von Raschke and his fearsome claw hold,
crew-cut Dick the Bruiser and crew-cut cousin the Crusher
winning World War II against their mortal enemies
the sneaky Japanese tag team. Arm bar. Drop kick.
The inescapable figure-four leg lock, known
to cripple the strongest men. I cheer for the good guys,
study their moves, yearn to fill out the form of real man.

Tending the Wound

Two weeks or so after the operation,
once the pain relaxes and boredom returns,
a resident takes me to the cast room
—not the one upstairs next to OR, but
the room on the first floor between X-ray
and the clinic. He picks up a hand-held
cast saw that sounds like it could cut through a tree
and holds it to my leg, less than an inch
above my skin. It vibrates wickedly
as he cuts out a window over the wound.
I watch him pull the plug out—bad smell bad,
no smell good—tear away the layers
of cotton, strip off the dressings, and expose
the cut. I feel air there for the first time
I can remember, but it doesn't look
like my skin, sliced then laced back together
so neatly. Doctor So-and-so pulls out
his instruments and digs in, snip, clip, yank,
and the first piece of fishing line is out.

The rest don't come so easily. I stop
watching as he digs and probes and fishes
for a couple dozen more threads
woven into my flesh. This, too, is
for my own good, but it goes on far
too long for this Christian martyr's need
for suffering. Once he finishes I catch
my breath. New bandage, cotton tucked over,
the plug goes back in. He slathers some rolls
of plaster on; we don't talk about this
latest trial. When he's done he cleans up,
blithely tells me I've passed another
milestone on the road to recovery.
It is the Sixties and I am young; I agree
to be fooled by this illusion of progress.

Sweet Soul Music

The piano is mostly in tune, and I listen
as Hoffmann bangs his heart and soul out. Chopsticks
is the other favorite tune. Thankfully the players
tire not too long after the audience does. Our real
music is on the radio—the Big Eighty-Nine,
W-L-S, each syllable exulted
by a choir bent on glory. The moon is blue,
love me do, I'll be true to you. But it's Telstar,
so far away, Detroit city, oh, how I want
to go home, homeward bound, I wish I was . . .
these are the songs that pierce my cover, that call my clan,
that cry in my voice in the can, in the closeted
hospital night. But I always want to walk like a man.

III. The Treatment

Return to the Ward

With all the times I've been in this place,
you'd think once I'd meet up again
with somebody I knew before—Bimbo
Weyers, say. Gerry Siwek. Even
Robert Walton. It never happens.
You just missed (fill-in-the-blank)—he left
two weeks ago. Last week. This morning.
He wanted me to say hello to you.
And so I start making a place
for myself again, learning names, faces,
remembering the rules and rhythms,
forgetting life outside, forgetting home.

Pater Noster

I am an orphan. Yes, Jesus loves me,
yes, my parents love me, and I live in the narrow space
between two worlds. I am not their son—
I am the son of Vulcan, the crippled god,
and down in his never-broken bones Jesus knows.
He is so sad, he knows I am lost.
My father makes a brace for me—he is good
with his hands—and I move through this world
like Jesus, reproach and inspiration to all.
For I am sent from on high—what do you worship?
Look upon me, then look within and know thy god.

Prep

You get out of school early the day before surgery.
They take you in the back and you take a long bath, scrub
everything, then they scrub you again with special soap.
Doesn't matter how big you are. Next they shave your leg
from the toes on up, even if the operation
is on your hip. Last time Miss Barb shaved some of my hair—
you know—lopped off a corner of the triangle. No need
to do that—they weren't going anywhere near there.
Don't know if it's growing back—under the cast, can't see
it. But there was no call to do that. None. Just meanness.

Before

I have been lying on this bed
for twenty hours. My leg is shaved.
My life is not yet over. No food
for eighteen hours, no water
for twelve. The life of the ward goes on
around me: the guys in the schoolroom,
aides and nurses bustling around.
Roll over. Somebody's mother in white
jabs my butt. The time is near.
I cannot sleep—have I ever slept well?
I lie on my back and try not
to count the holes in the ceiling tiles.

A year later an intern in green
rolls a stretcher up to my bed; I scoot
on. He straps me down. He does not talk.
The stretcher's rubber tires whiz down the hall;
ceiling tiles zip by overhead.
At the elevator we wait. I smell
the reeking kitchen, rank but not yet so
sickening as it will be. Silverware
clatters in the staff dining room—round
tables, white tablecloths. In the slow
elevator I watch the smooth ceiling.

At once we're outside the operating room.
I forgot to be thirsty. The intern parks
me outside the open doors. I can't see
in, but I hear them, padded shoes across
the tile floor, clanking instruments—scalpels?
A voice I can't make out—and whistling.
Someone is whistling. I'm strapped down out here
waiting to be a train wreck, and some chipper lark
is whistling, making it up as he goes.
There are holes in the ceiling tiles here too,
and I want him to stop whistling. I can take
the clank of the tools, the sunshine through glass brick
windows, the waiting, the big sharp moon light,
the spike in the arm, the mask, the gas,
the spinning, choking, puking—I can take it all.
Anything but the whistling. Stop. Please.

Fear at Thirteen

On your back on the narrow table, one leg shaved
to the hip, gown folded up to your ribs, nurse fishing
for a vein to start the IV, huge dome of light
close overhead, gas mask nearby, instruments
clanking, green masks showing only bandit eyes,
blue-eyed nurse washing up your leg with Betadine,
hatchet men waiting to cut you, and what you fear most
in all the world is that you'll pop a boner
and die embarrassed on this green yet sterile field.

From the Surgeons: Drs. Sofield, Louis, Hark, Alfini, Millar, Baehr, Bevan-Thomas, Tsatsos, Ericson, and Bennan

6-10-60. History. This child is the second of three
children—the other two are perfectly normal. He was the product
of a normal pregnancy and delivery. At birth it was noted
that the left lower extremity was shorter than the right. The child
had a fragmentation and rodding of the left femur
for stimulation of bone growth. Prior to that procedure a 2" discrepancy
existed. This procedure was repeated in 1957 and again in 1958. Prior
to the procedure in 1958 a 2" discrepancy was again noted. The child's
early development was normal. He has, of course, been periodically set back
in his physical progress because of the surgical procedures.

6-10-60. Physical Examination. Head: There is nothing
abnormal about the head. Left lower extremity: There appears
to be only a very moderate degree of atrophy in the left thigh, but
this is explainable on the basis of his surgical procedures.
Gait is moderately abnormal but caused only
by the leg length discrepancy.

7-28-61. History. He began sitting at six months of age, walked
at one year, and began talking at about one year of age. There have been
some periods of regression following the early surgical procedures. The boy
is attending school and is apparently well adjusted.

7-28-61. Physical Examination. Examination reveals a slight
compensatory scoliosis. This is corrected by equalization of leg lengths.
This boy walks with a left short leg limp. He is able to run without difficulty,
and can hop on his right foot, but he is unable to hop on his left foot.
When performing the duck waddle his left leg leads the right.

12-7-62. Neurological Examination. Deep tendon reflexes
are physiological. There is a slight diminution of the left knee jerk
as contrasted with that on the right. No sensory loss nor pathologic reflexes.

8-28-63. Progress Notes. The mother relates that the boy has been
stumbling more and more in recent weeks. His quadriceps are
quite weak, probably from the multiple surgical procedures
done on this thigh. Quadriceps are rather bound down at the knee.
The leg length discrepancy is 3" and it is very difficult
to have a satisfactory shoe lift on this dimension. A long leg brace
was ordered with knee locks and with a 2" pylon extension.

11-8-63. Progress Notes. This boy has received his long leg brace
with the caliper extension today. The brace is satisfactory,
except for the fact that the ankle joint is rigid and
he has a great deal of difficulty getting his trousers on and off
and needs to split the seams.

8-14-64. Progress Notes. This child who is almost 10 years of age
is wearing a long leg brace with a stilt on it, but the mother says
that he objects to this and apparently is undergoing considerable
emotional disturbance. The mother has noticed this since his return
from the hospital at which time he had a repeat fragmentation and rodding.

4-7-67. Physical Examination. Lower extremities: Circumference:
There is obvious atrophy of the left thigh: This cannot
be accurately compared with the right because of the shortness
of the extremity and the dislocation of the patella.

6-6-69. History. The child is in the ninth grade and does fair
and goes to a regular school.

10-30-70. Progress Notes. Final Discharge. The patient is essentially
unchanged since last visit. His leg lengths measured to the heel
on the right measures 101 and 86 on the left from the anterior superior
iliac spine. He has occasional episodes of pain. He is still
wearing the long leg brace with the high lift below
and there was no indication on the mother's part that she plans
on having anything done in the near future.

The Coliseum

On your first Monday inside you get the treatment.
They skip you on rounds, then when everyone else
relaxes and gets on with the day, you are led
through the halls—no one looks at you straight on—
to the small room

behind the coliseum. There you doff your clothes—all
of them—for the bareback gown and G-string. No cheating,
no underwear, no, nothing that the masters wear—
the keepers enforce. You sit in the cold and listen
for a clue about what lies

ahead—but nothing. At once pushed on stage, gown whisked
off—even that gone—you blink in the cold light
till they poke and prod you to walk their gauntlet
of humiliation, their parade of shame,
before this pride

of professionals, lords of the hospital, cold-eyed
white coats trained to find your flaws, focus on failings,
who measure your meat minutely. You are a specimen
for study, a toy, a puzzle—they speak to each other as if
you are unconscious

already, but for commands: stand, bend, walk this way,
on this leg, on that. They forget about you for long
stretches, a kind of mercy, while you stand bare naked,
while they rehearse and renew your shame. When you are numb
through, they tire

of you, they turn you loose. You are so happy to be out
from scrutiny, so happy even for ugly clothes, for underwear,
so happy to get back to your pen, back to the ward where you are
one among many, just another kid,
almost a person again.

Standard Operating Procedure

Take your very best electric drill, the variable speed, reversible one.
Pick out a five sixty-fourths inch bit. Dunk
it in alcohol and put it in the drill. Close the chuck,
squeeze the trigger. Working OK? Good.

Take a young boy and lie him down on your work bench.
Tell him this is for his own good, this will hurt
you more than him. Tell him. Then press the drill
to his thigh and squeeze the trigger. Keep drilling
until you get through the bone. He won't like it much; children
are like that. If he squirms, render him unconscious. Ether will do.
He'll throw up later, but that will be somebody else's problem.
You have work to do. It might go quicker if you slice
open the thigh with a knife—like you'd cut veal—
through skin and muscle right down to the bone.
Now your drill should get a good purchase. Bore four holes
in that little bone. If you like you can clamp the leg
in a vise so it doesn't slide around. Bust a chunk
of bone the rest of the way out; chisel it if you have
to. No shame in not using bare hands. Wire the bone in
there backwards, and sew him up with fishing line or thread.
While he's still out wrap him up good in plaster so he can't move
for ten or twelve weeks. Don't forget to clean your drill.

He'll be out for a while, but dose him with morphine
for his trouble. He won't remember much; kids are like animals
that way. Anyway, you had a job to do. You'll go on
to many new operations; soon, you won't even remember that leg,
let alone that boy. Tears and pain are standard operating
procedure, and you have other problems now to solve.

Visitation

The holiness twins in habitual black
and white await as I round the corner.
No cliff to jump off, my legs are pudding,
I crawl into my cast to hide with the hair
and the dried skin, but they see me—by their eyes,
by their prayers, I am pinned to my cross. I am no suicide,
I am no Jesus, no Socrates, please sir, I am
a feral boy, raised by wolves and the kindness
of strangers. Yes, I put out my hand for punishment,
yes, I bare my loins, I bow to superior force.
I am shaved and scorned and starved and scarred.
If the gods do not like my sacrifice,
if Jesus looks away bored, Lord, to you I will give
my other leg. I am not worthy to receive you,
only rend my flesh and my soul shall be healed.

All We Do

All we do is wait—wait for the doctor
to come, wait for the pain med, wait for school
to end, wait for visiting hours,
wait for visitors to leave, stitches out,
clean clothes, lunch, the Monkees on TV, mail,
that Notre Dame quarterback one Christmas
who never showed, wait to walk again, wait
for good songs on the radio, to sleep
in a real dark room, to talk on the phone,
to be alone, wait until they send us home.

Hip Spica

The well-made hip
spica cast weighs
something less than
a ton—at least mine
does. I can see the
toes on my left foot,
then it is nothing but
plaster up past my
bellybutton. They leave
my crotch free, barely,
but I can do everything
I need to. Except scratch.
Itching is forever. I even
wear underwear—no
G-string for me. I take
aim and toss the briefs—big ones—over my left foot. Right
foot lines them up, pulls that elastic band up where I can grab
with my left hand. Off is easy—reverse process, no aiming
needed. I'll use a urinal—never a bedpan, splayed out turtle on
its back. I'd hold it forever. When they let me out of bed I drag
myself to a stall. The doctors would shit if they knew—nurses
too. But I don't belong to this clunky cast—it belongs to me.

Banana Cart

Not like a coffin, no—a long flat wooden box,
no pads, no top, to transport us round the ward, not
to the great beyond that we never talk about.
Adjustable backrest, wheelchair wheels, push yourself
around, wheelchair for those who do not fit
into wheelchairs, wheelie machine—my balance is
exquisite, if no nurses are watching
I can do laps around the ward, front wheels high
in the air, no hip spica can keep me down.

New Cast

Sometimes blood would seep from the wound
into damp plaster, and evening rust
would mingle with whitewash white,
reminding all who cared to look just
what well-intentioned violence
lay under that stiff, brittle trust.

Post-Op

Waking up in a bin of cotton—
you just want to clear this stuff from your eyes,
your ears, most of all your mouth.. The room
jumps like it touched something hot, spins away,
and you puke into this curved steel basin
by your mouth. Bitter, but you feel better
as you spit the taste out. Mrs. Spoerl
comes over, and her perfume makes
you want to puke again, but you don't.
She wipes your mouth—how are you feeling?—
takes the basin away. You think
maybe that's not a good idea,
but she's back with a fresh one before you
can puke again. Her hand on your forehead,
it feels so cool, so good and normal that
you don't want to have to puke again but
oh God it's another bucketful—
it feels like a gallon but you never
fill that emesis basin, thank God.

She takes your temp, checks your blood pressure,
gives you a shot for pain. And then you're gone.
This heavy ocean throws you up
on shore from time to time. You puke, suck
on ice chips, and loll there like a dinghy
in the trough of a wave. The afternoon
waltzes, when awake you notice the cast—
it feels hot—the pain, your mouth, your gut,
your head. This is not fun. The puke pan
feels good against your skin. You cling to it,
a straw against this pitching sea. You felt
fine this morning; now you can't quite recall
your name, but you remember Mrs. Spoerl,
Mrs. Spoerl, Mrs. Spoerl. Recovery room.

Late afternoon they take you back
to the ward, wheel your bed along the halls,
the lights overhead flashing as you pass
underneath. Nothing feels good. The guys
and nurses are solicitous on your
return, but the ward is bright, busy,
jarring, and you just want to be alone,
unconscious, something. Off and on you are
unconscious, and, whoever is with you,
you are alone. And it hurts. No one
can share this, and you know it in your marrow
when you're wide awake at midnight,
for the first time since morning, and now you know
how much it hurts, how badly your bones
mistreated, how alone you can be
in a room with fifteen others. Night nurse
out of sight, and you don't want to call out
like you've heard hundreds of quavering voices
do before, you throw your head side to side
because it takes your mind off how much
your leg hurts and then you hear it anyway,

God damn it! That's your voice quaking *Nurse?*
And then it happens again *Nurse?* and you
just can't help it out it comes *Nurse!* And now
your humiliation is complete.
Everyone crumbles after surgery.
The nurse comes, she brings ice chips, a shot
for the pain, and you breathe again, relax
your neck as you're released to tomorrow.

Abecedarius Hospitaler

A small sea of white coats, mouths and eyeballs
Bobs, waves, watches the specimen on stage,
Chatters about the boy who would be so
Durably cold if he were here, but he
Enters the sea, dons a lab coat for style,
For warmth, for safety on the sea, and the sea
Gabbles on, boring into what's left of
Him on the stage, washing away all down to all-
Important bone, washing away shame, joy,
Jealousy, to get down to the driftwood,
Keeping the rest suspended in cold storage,
Left to stand unsupported while we look,
Mutter, mull what to do with this one, this
New problem, this puzzle with a name. Cut
Or not cut—that's never the question—it's
Places to cut, which bones to saw first—that's the
Question, but this sea is dense and the mist
Rolls in, it always rolls in, and whatever
Safety the white coat provides melts down
To nothing, the sea is no safer than
Under the cold spotlight—it still ends in
Vomit and pain, but for me, not for them,
Whatever they decide they keep their coats,
X-rays, tools and tricks, and I know my place—
You're up there, kid—and my job—to be the
Zoo animal, so I pace, I shiver, I don't cry.

Homecoming

He had been like us years before; now
he is back to revisit the scene
of his abasement and transformation.
He came back to show himself how far
he'd come. To touch the child he was once.
To stand transfigured before us who know.
He looks so awkward—who am I to call him
awkward—he looks timeless, at sea
on his eternity. He limps, doesn't he?
Does he see us when the shirt-and-tie
shows him around? Or does he see his moment,
his ghostly limbs as he shows us the future?

Biological Determinism

Jockeying for position at the starting line
in our casts and hormones, bad haircuts, wheelchairs,
crutches, banana carts, awaiting word from heaven,
from the Girls Ward, we're tense and ready or already
giving up when our nurse fires her starter pistol.
We race up the hallway, bumping and thrashing
toward our biological destiny.

Only one can win whatever it is out there
at the other end of the dark hall, only one,
and we push and jostle and trick each other
to be the only one, to get there first, to claim our rightful prize:
to park next to the bed of the prettiest crippled girl
in the hospital. *You boys were horrible*
to those girls, swarming around that one like flies

and crushing all the others. Like we ourselves were crushed,
crippled prizes, chipped loving cups, slightly cracked goblets,
chairs with three pretty good legs. Lisa was our holy grail—
forgive me, Darlene, forgive me, Wanda—she was the light
we yearned to buzz around, the screen we smacked our heads against.
One night I got off free and clear, strong in shoulder and arm,
I left them all behind and sailed into the Girls Ward alone,

the only one. But I was too soon, my prize lying down,
I couldn't find her, didn't recognize her until
she was surrounded by those who finally caught up.
My crippled love was lost, is lost still, and all I have
to give is slightly salty on the skin, the musk that comes
and goes, my twisted leanings, my violent falls,
and getting up, again, again, again.

About the Author

Jim Ferris was born and raised in Cook County, Illinois. He attended parochial and public schools, including brief stints as a student of Chicago's Spalding School for Crippled Children. A former newspaper reporter, televison producer, and gas station pump jockey, Ferris has won awards for his teaching as well as his writing. He currently teaches disability studies and communication arts at the University of Wisconsin–Madison.